SISTER WENDY BECKETT

A CHILD'S
BOOK OF
PRAYER *in* ART

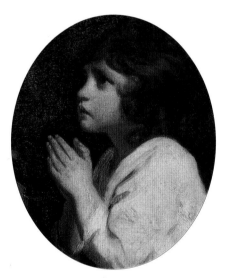

"LOOKING AT ART IS ONE WAY
OF LISTENING TO GOD."
—*Sister Wendy Beckett*

A DORLING KINDERSLEY BOOK

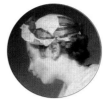

First American Edition, 1995
2 4 6 8 10 9 7 5 3

Published in the United States by
Dorling Kindersley Publishing, Inc. 95 Madison Avenue
New York, New York 10016

Published in Great Britain by Dorling Kindersley Limited.
Distributed by Houghton Mifflin Company, Boston.

Library of Congress Cataloging-in-Publication Data
Beckett, Wendy.
A child's book of prayer in art / by Wendy Beckett. —1st American ed.
p.   cm.
ISBN 1-56458-875-0
1. Children—Prayer-books and devotions—English. 2. Art and religion—Juvenile
literature. [1. Prayer books and devotions.   2. Art appreciation.] I. Title
BV4870.B387   1995   94-40362
242'.62—dc20   CIP
                                                  AC

Color reproduction by G.R.B. Graphica, Verona
Printed in Italy by New Interlitho

SISTER WENDY BECKETT

A CHILD'S
BOOK OF
PRAYER *in* ART

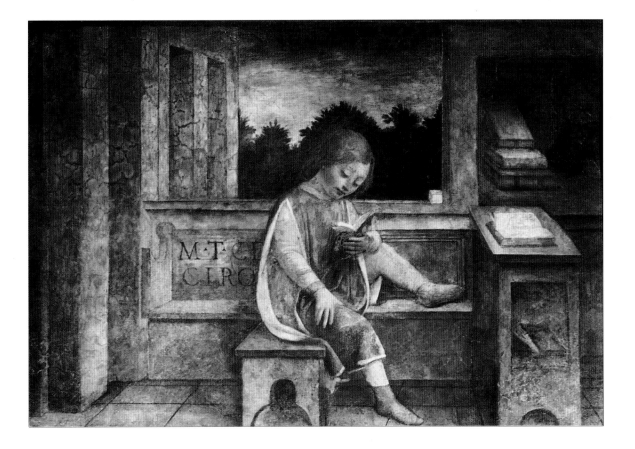

DORLING KINDERSLEY

LONDON • NEW YORK • STUTTGART

SISTER WENDY'S NOTE TO PARENTS AND TEACHERS

This book is really self-contained and, in many cases, the best thing for an adult to do is simply stay clear—let children get on with the book alone. But for some children (especially younger children), there is definitely a place for adult involvement.

All I can suggest is that you take this book seriously. We should not discuss the ideas in this book with children unless we are sincerely trying to live in love and truth ourselves. Failure does not matter, but cynicism matters, despair matters, lack of commitment matters. Children learn more from what we are than from what we say.

But it is not only children who will discover something of value in this book. The demands of goodness and of real human integrity remain unaltered throughout our lives. There is nothing in this book that is not as wholly valid for the 90-year-old as for the nine-year-old.

May all of us who use this book, of whatever age or religion, be prepared to listen to our God.

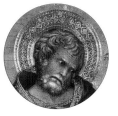

CONTENTS

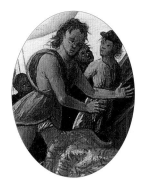

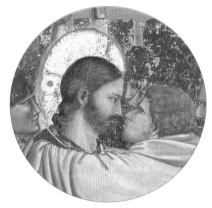
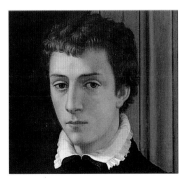
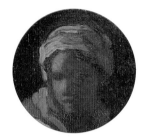
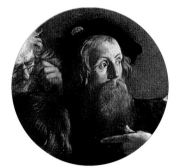

INTRODUCTION

This book is about happiness with God. It is about knowing from our own selves, without needing anybody to tell us, what God is like. God is total love—someone who is never cross, never uncaring, never absent from us, and always protective and understanding. God is sad when we will not live in truth and goodness, because then we suffer, and God is always trying to draw us into happiness.

Learning what God is like is called prayer. When we pray, we open ourselves to the love that is God, absolutely certain that God will hear us and help us to change. We usually think that praying is talking to God, and so it often is. But even more often it is listening to God, even though we cannot hear words. Instead we shall find ourselves simply knowing what God is like and what we ought to do. God will teach us silently if we are listening.

Looking at art is one way of listening to God. Look at each painting in this book carefully. Each one needs time. As we look, we must think about each painting, and stay quietly before it, giving God space to enter our hearts and change them, to make them good and fill them with happiness.

So, take your time. Look at only one picture at a time. Stay with it and let the picture draw you into itself and reveal itself to you. There is no one right way to look. Different people will see and understand different things. We cannot understand unless we are truly serious and sincere—but if we try to listen and learn, God will always help us, until we are true all the way through, as God is.

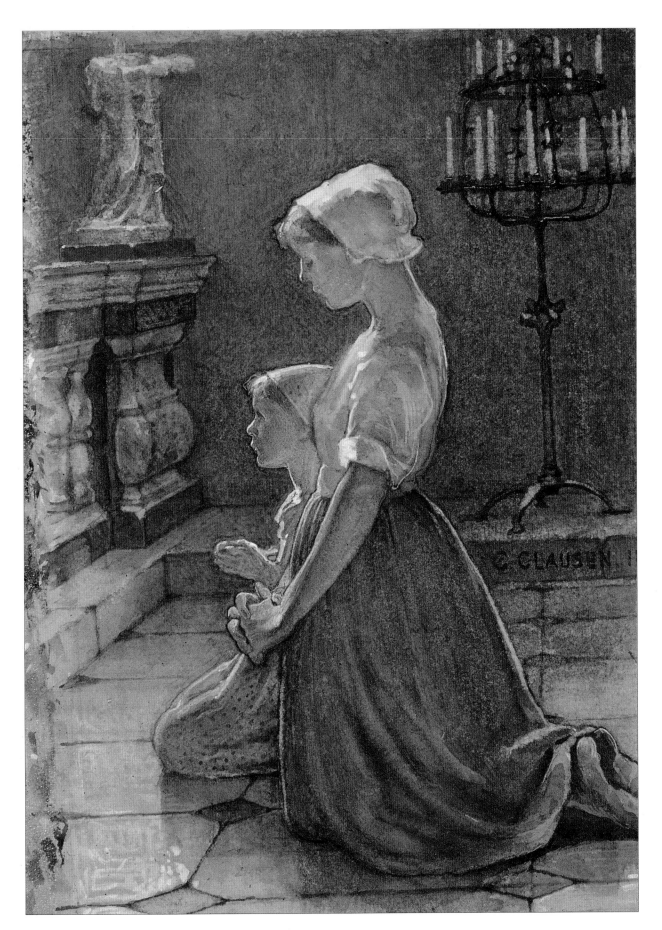

FRENCH PEASANT GIRLS PRAYING *Sir George Clausen*

RESPECT

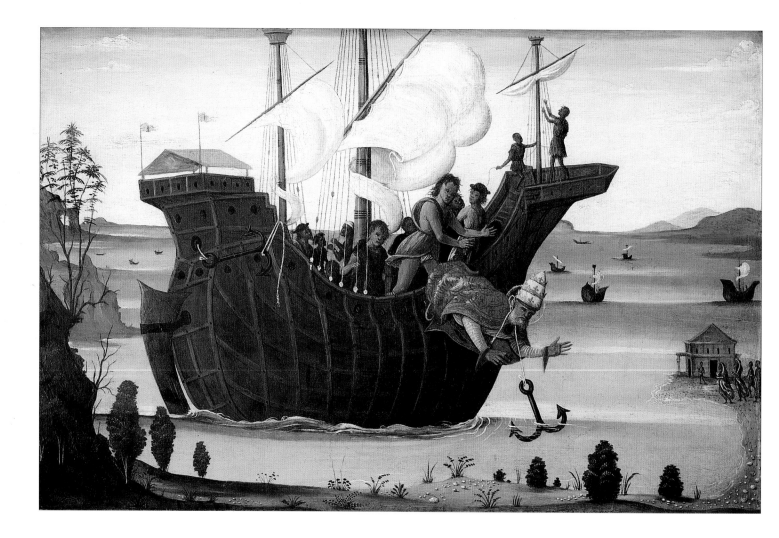

THE MARTYRDOM OF SAINT CLEMENT

Bernardino Fungai
This painting is one panel of an altarpiece that Fungai
painted at the beginning of the sixteenth century.

SOMETIMES WE HEAR PEOPLE TALKING ABOUT SIN. TO SIN REALLY MEANS TO PUT WHAT WE WANT before the rights and needs of others. Doing this is wrong because it means that we stay small and mean and concerned with ourselves, and never grow large of heart. This picture shows some men throwing an old man called Pope Clement into the sea. They have tied an anchor around his neck so that his body will stay on the bottom of the sea and never be found. They are killing him because his religion is not the same as theirs.

> "Teach me to respect other people and the way they live and the things they believe. Help me never to be cruel. Help me to trust other people and leave them their freedom to be different."

The murderers do not respect Pope Clement's right to live or his right to have his own religion. God loves and respects everyone and grieves to see such cruelty. God made the sea recede so that Pope Clement's friends could find his body, which was lying in that little temple at the side of the painting.

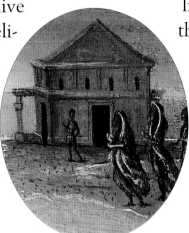

It is such a lovely day. The sea is like a bright mirror reflecting the blue of the sky. Everything in the picture is beautiful except the hearts of those who do not respect another man and his religion. We can all be cruel and hateful like this, but we can ask God to teach us how to respect everyone.

LOVE

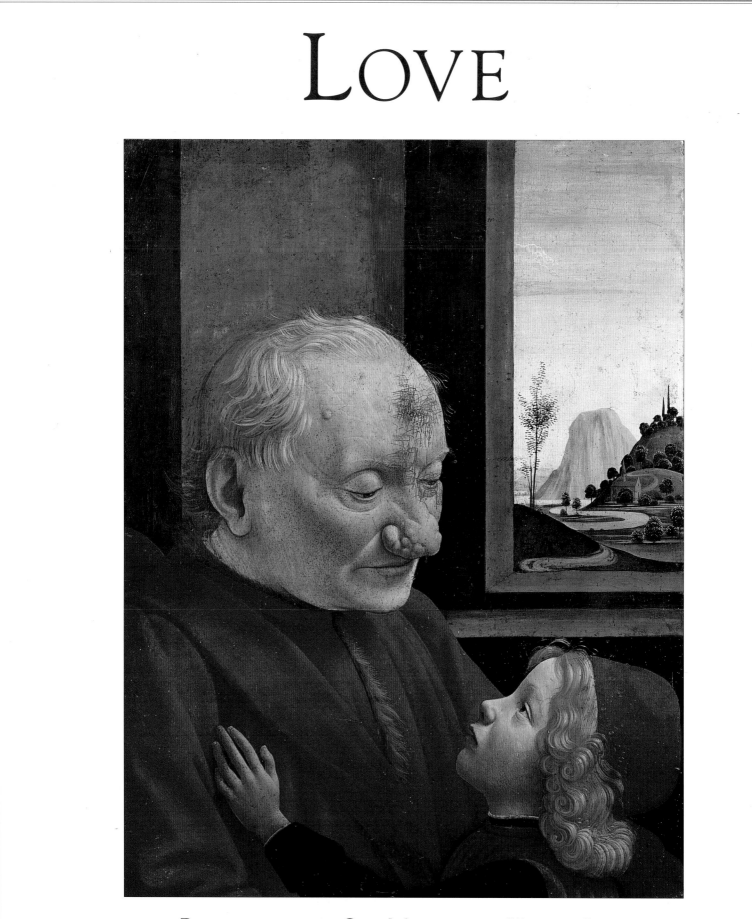

PORTRAIT OF AN OLD MAN AND A YOUNG BOY
Domenico Ghirlandaio
Ghirlandaio painted this tender scene
around the year 1490.

THE OLD MAN IN THIS PAINTING LOOKS STRANGE—HIS NOSE IS COVERED IN warts and blisters. Yet a young boy looks straight up at him with a look of trust and love. It would hurt the man if the boy was afraid of him, or laughed at him, or was in any way unkind. There is a lovely view through the window of a tall, feathery tree and a road winding up a mountain into the distance. There is a silvery lake and a pale blue sky. But the little boy is not fretting to get outside. He knows that the old man needs him.

> "Teach me to accept other people with love as you do. Help me to take other people as they are and never be cruel or unkind, whatever they look like."

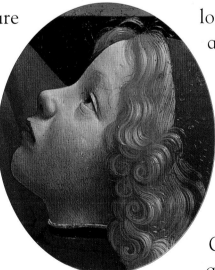

The boy and the man are not talking. They are just looking at each other with love. The boy puts his hand on the man's chest and the man probably has his arms around the boy. This is how we should treat other people: gently and kindly. This is how God treats us. God loves us no matter what we are like. We might think we look all right on the outside, but God can see through to our inner selves, too. Sometimes these are not very nice. But even if we have nasty things inside us, God takes us as we are and goes on holding us tight.

FAMILY

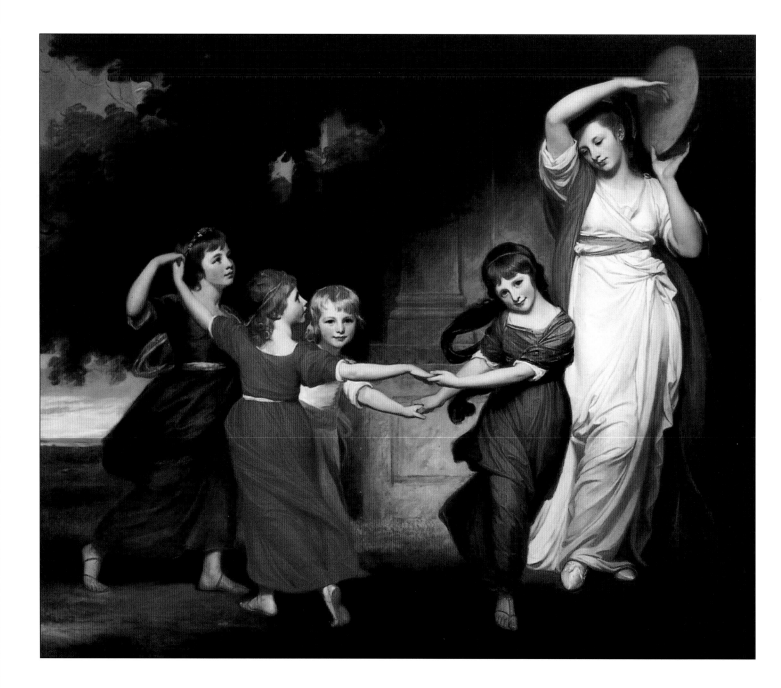

THE GOWER FAMILY
George Romney
Romney worked in London and painted this family in 1776-77.

HERE WE SEE FOUR CHILDREN DANCING WHILE THEIR SISTER, ANNE (THEIR half-sister really), plays music for them. When brothers and sisters fight, it is as if nasty music is being played in their family. But this family is very happy together, making sweet music. The older children do not leave out the younger ones. Anne does not mind that she is not a part of the dance itself because she is helping to keep time for the others. The younger children hold hands and quietly enjoy being with Anne.

> " Please help me to love my brothers and sisters and be kind to them. Please make our life together as happy and helpful as this dance. "

The family does not seem to be in a very comfortable place. There is a big tree that casts a lot of dark shadow, which even looks like it could be smoke. The shadow blots out all of the sunshine, and the stone wall behind the children looks cold.

But families need to hold together most of all when there are dark shadows around them and things are not going very well. The children in this painting are all helping one another keep warm and happy in this dark and chilly place.

UNDERSTANDING

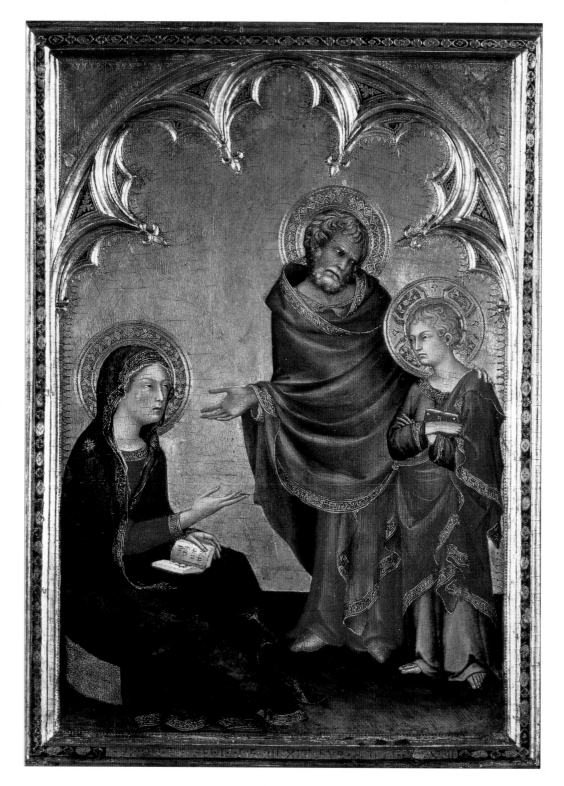

CHRIST DISCOVERED IN THE TEMPLE
Simone Martini
Martini painted this colorful small scene in 1342.

SOMETIMES WE THINK THAT PEOPLE WHO LOVE ONE ANOTHER ALWAYS UNDERSTAND one another. No family ever shared more love than Joseph, his wife Mary, and Jesus, her son. Yet even they did not always understand one another. Jesus had been lost for three days in Jerusalem and Mary and Joseph were terribly worried, looking for him everywhere. When they found him, sitting in the Temple, he was astonished that they had not known he would be in God's house.

"Please help me to understand other people and not to be too upset when they do not understand me. Help me to realize that love and anger can go together."

Mary is sad and annoyed: how could Jesus have caused them so much anxiety? But Jesus is also sad and annoyed: how could his mother, so close to God and to him, not have known where to look for him? Both feel that they are in the right, and poor Joseph is left in the middle, trying to make peace. In a moment, they will forgive each other. But the pain of misunderstanding will not go away. They are learning a great lesson. We must always say, "I may be wrong," whenever we are certain that we are right. Here, both are "right" and both are "wrong," as often happens in misunderstandings.

15

LEARNING

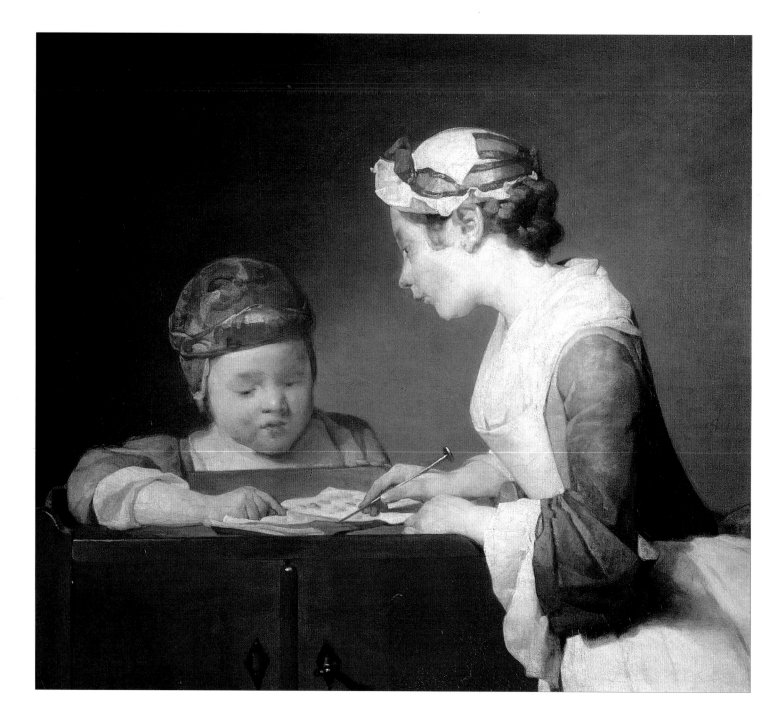

THE YOUNG SCHOOLMISTRESS
Jean-Baptiste-Siméon Chardin
Chardin liked simple everyday scenes such as this one,
which he painted around the year 1740.

SOME PEOPLE LIKE SCHOOL AND SOME DO NOT, BUT EVERYBODY NEEDS AN EDUCATION. WE MUST learn many things, or else we can never fully enter into grown-up life. We cannot learn unless we listen carefully to our teachers. This child is really listening to what his teacher is saying. The child does not seem to understand his lesson—his face is anxious and the teacher looks impatient. Perhaps she is his big sister and he is being taught on his own at home. It is not only in the classroom, or from qualified teachers, that we learn about the world.

" Help me to really listen to my teachers and not to waste my time at school. Help me to listen to everybody who is good and wise and not think that I already know everything. "

School is very important. What we do with our lives may depend upon how well we listen to our teachers and let them show us how the world works. This child is truly trying to grasp what his teacher is showing him and he is not giving up just because he finds it difficult.

If we listen to the people we meet, especially wise and good people, and if we ask them thoughtful questions and try to understand what they say, we can become wise ourselves. This is not just true when we are young—the wisest people continue to learn all their lives.

FORGIVENESS

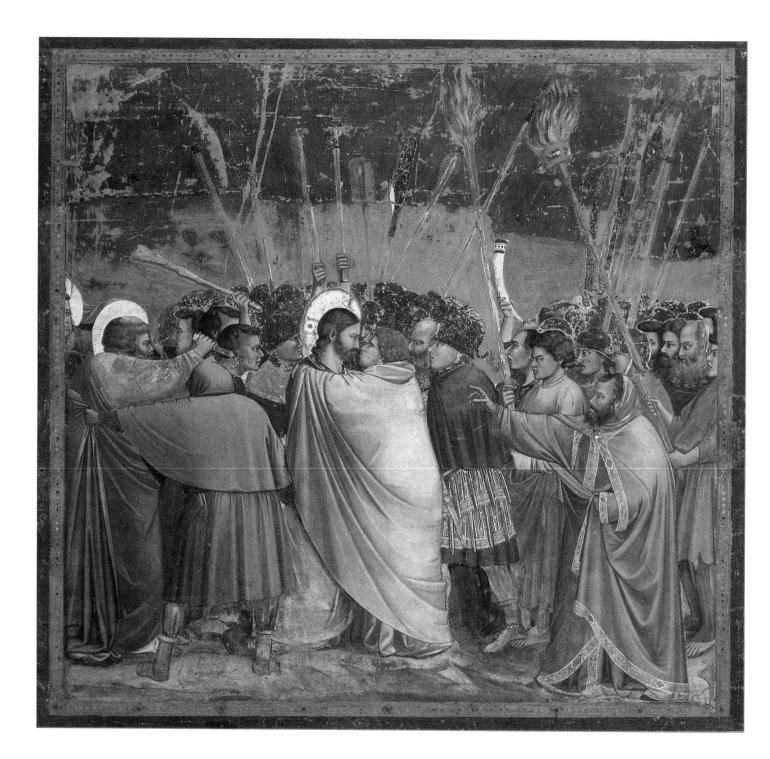

THE KISS OF JUDAS
Giotto di Bondone
It is thought that Giotto painted this dramatic scene
between 1304 and 1310.

GIOTTO SHOWS US TWO MEN

HUGGING EACH OTHER, BUT SOMETHING IS wrong. There are lots of other men around, creating an air of great tension. The story of this painting is very sad. Jesus and Judas were friends, and Jesus had chosen Judas to be one of his disciples. Jesus's enemies gave Judas 30 gold pieces to show them where Jesus was hiding so they could kill him. Judas said they would recognize Jesus because Judas would kiss him. So Judas is doing a terrible thing: betraying his friend for money.

> "Never let me betray anyone, and if I do, please help me to say at once that I am sorry. Teach me that God always forgives, however dreadful I have been."

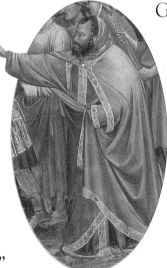

Jesus knows exactly what his friend has done, but what does he say to him? Does he say, "Go away, God is angry with you, you are a wicked man"? No. Jesus lets Judas kiss him and says sadly, "My friend, why have you come here?" So to Jesus, Judas is still "my friend."

God always forgives, but we have to accept God's forgiveness, too, by saying we are sorry and trying to do better. Judas would not even try to accept God's forgiveness and start again—he gave up and killed himself, not believing that God always, totally and unfailingly, forgives.

CHOOSING HEAVEN

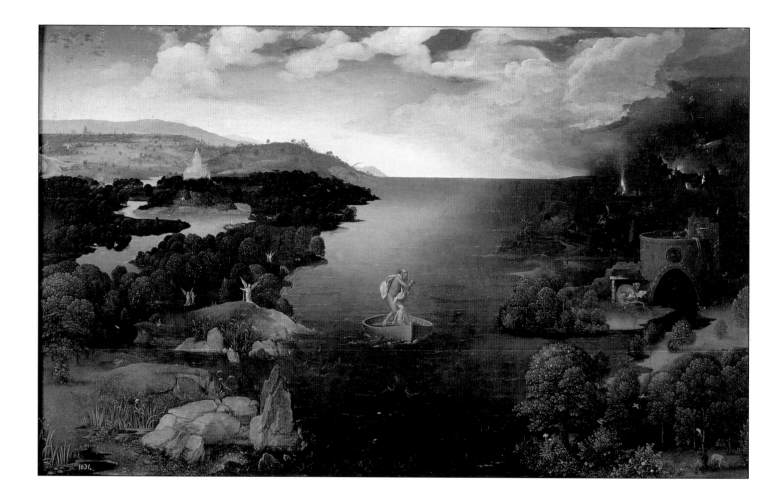

CHARON CROSSING THE STYX
Joachim Patinir
Patinir painted fantastic landscapes such as this one in
the late fifteenth and early sixteenth centuries.

THERE IS AN ANCIENT GREEK STORY ABOUT A MAN CALLED CHARON. WHEN PEOPLE died, he took them across the river of death to the next world. Here, Patinir imagines the next world as two different worlds—one of happiness and one of sadness: heaven and hell. On one side of the river is the world of sorrow, with darkness, fire, and horrible demons. On the other side is the world of happiness, with calm lakes, clear light, and welcoming angels. In the middle of the painting, a tiny, naked person sits in Charon's boat.

> " When I am feeling sad or angry, let me be brave and overcome my feelings. Teach me that I can choose to be happy. "

We do not need Charon's boat—we can choose for ourselves whether we live in happiness or sorrow. When we are unhappy and things are going wrong, we are on the "hell" side of the river. But we do not have to stay there. We can ignore our bad luck and live on the other side of the river, in happiness. It is

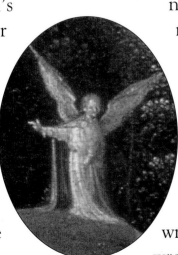

not as if Charon is steadily rowing us toward unhappiness—sad feelings are not forced upon us. Although we cannot help feeling sad, we *can* help staying sad. We can choose to smile, and if we smile our feelings will change. There is nothing wrong with feeling bad, but it is wrong not to try and get over it.

TRUE HAPPINESS

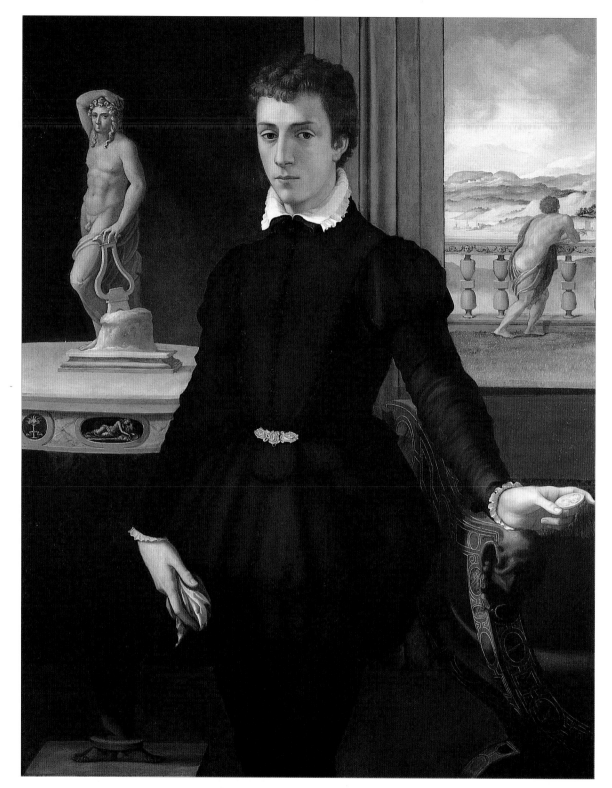

PORTRAIT OF A YOUNG MAN
Alessandro Allori
Allori painted this refined portrait in 1561.

THE YOUNG MAN IN THIS PICTURE DOES NOT SEEM TO BE LOOKING AT US—I WONDER WHAT he is thinking of? He is obviously very rich. His clothes are all black, but they are made of expensive materials such as velvet. His collar is crisp with a frilled edge. All around the young man are signs that he loves beautiful things. There is a marble statue standing on a decorated table, a splendid chair is at his side, and he is holding a precious medal. Behind him, we can see a painting of a man with hardly any clothes on.

> "Make me free of heart and show me how happiness comes more from giving than from having a lot of things. Help me not to be greedy and not to think that possessions matter too much."

The half-dressed man is looking longingly out to the distant mountains and the sea. Perhaps he will jump over the edge of the balcony, leap into the sea, and enjoy his freedom. The young man has a rather sad look on his face. His wealth has not necessarily brought him happiness.

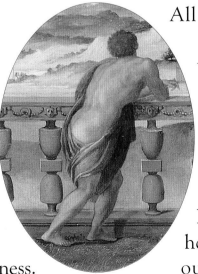

All of the lovely things that surround him leave the young man lonely. He may want to escape, like the man in the picture on the wall. We sometimes think we would be different if only we had lots of things. But nothing makes us truly happy except being true to ourselves with God's help.

THINKING

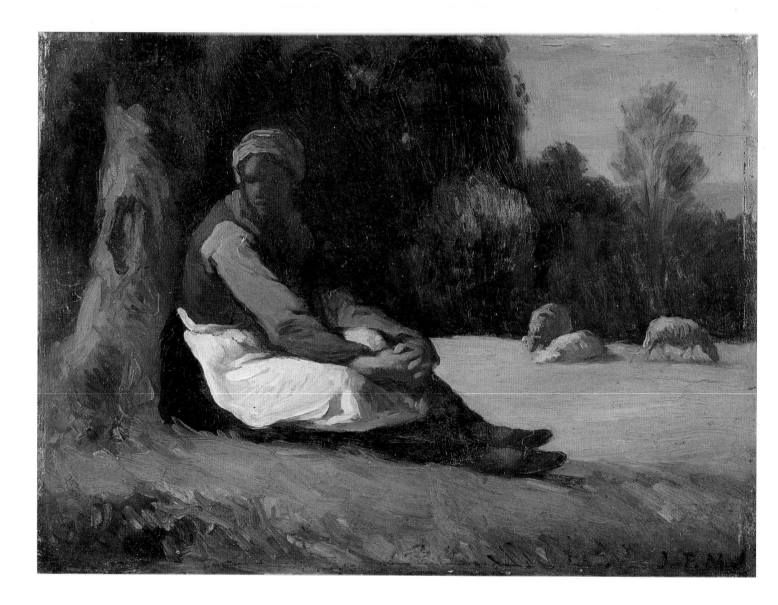

SEATED SHEPHERDESS
Jean-François Millet
In the late 1840s, Millet painted a number of pictures of
ordinary country people such as this young shepherdess.

THIS GIRL HAS A VERY BORING JOB. ALL DAY SHE HAS TO SIT OUTSIDE AND LOOK after the sheep. She is very poor, and we might think that she is very lonely. There is nobody else here but the sheep, and she has nobody to talk to and no games to play. But Millet makes us see that she is perfectly content. The meadow is full of peace and warmth. Even the sheep are at rest in the sunshine. We cannot see her face very clearly because it is in the shade, but we can see her hands. They are lying quietly upon her knees.

"Help me to understand that everyone needs a little silence in their lives. Give me the strength to search for a silent time every day so that I can think things out peacefully and quietly, and learn to live wisely."

The shepherdess is using her time to think. We all need a quiet time like this. If we are always noisy and active and restless, we are only living with one part of ourselves. Deep inside us are our real selves, which make the choices that matter and think things out. Nobody can tell us how to live—we all have to work out the wisest way for ourselves. God waits to help us. If we are silent, God can guide us to the best way. This picture shows us someone who is quietly thinking and praying, and letting God show her what is right.

25

DETERMINATION

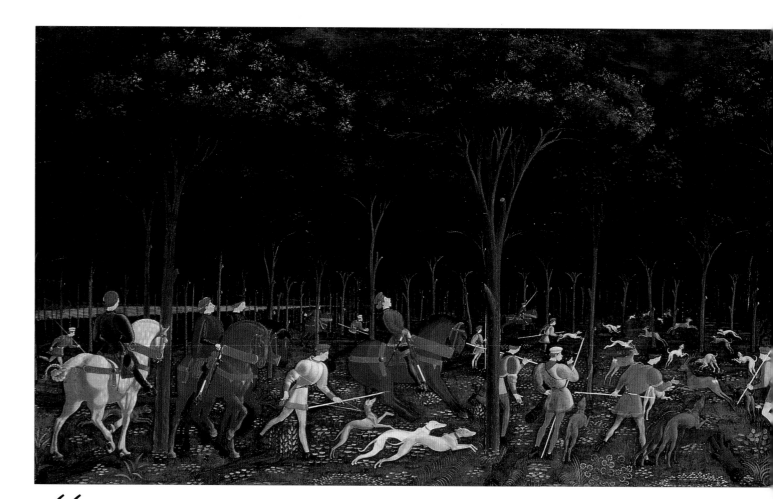

“Strengthen my will so that I can make decisions and stick to them. Show me the things that really matter to me and help me to use my energy in the best possible way.”

THIS WHOLE PICTURE IS ALIVE WITH MOVEMENT. WE SEE MEN ON HORSEBACK AND ON FOOT RACING INTO THE FOREST WITH hunting dogs. They must be hunting something deep within the trees, because the dogs and men are taking no notice of the stags they have already frightened. What this painting shows is concentration. The hunters are all aiming for a central object that we cannot see. They all know—the dogs as much as the men—exactly what they want. They want to catch the creature that none of them can see, but all know is there.

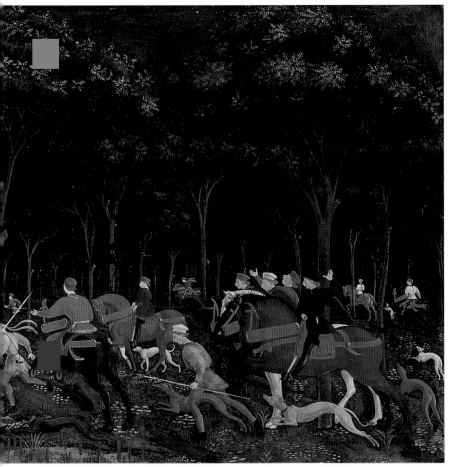

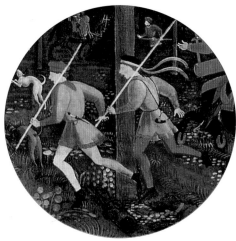

HUNT BY NIGHT
Paolo Uccello
It is thought that Uccello painted this carefully composed scene between 1466 and 1467.

Every part of the hunting party is centered on that invisible creature. Nothing in the scene is directed away from it. The great rows of trees do not stop the hunters. Even the lovely grass with the white flowers all around cannot tempt them to rest.

It is a wonderful thing to know what we want and concentrate on finding it. If we direct all our energy toward our goal, we shall reach it, however distant it may be. God will help us if it is a good thing we want, but we have to want it with all our hearts.

SELFLESSNESS

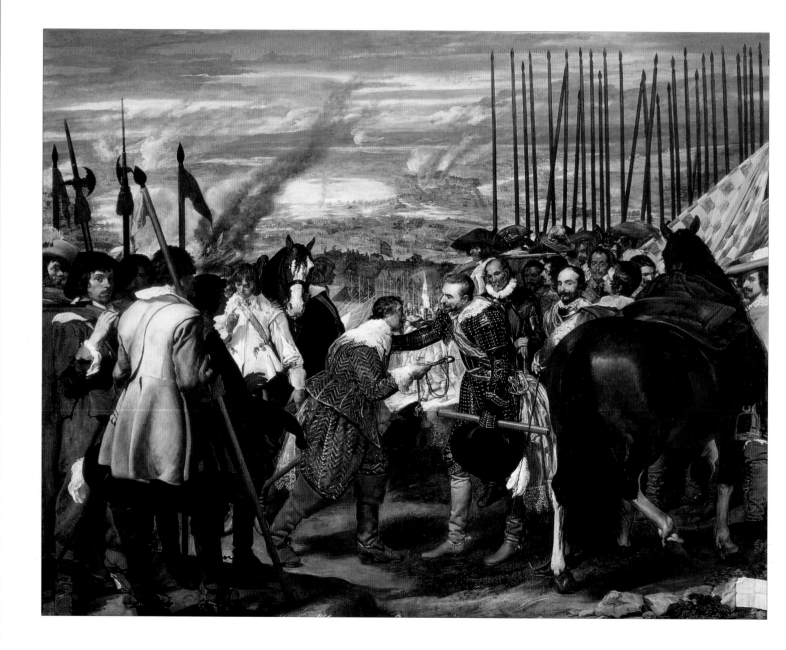

THE SURRENDER OF BREDA
Diego Velázquez
The Spanish artist Velázquez painted this enormous
picture between 1634 and 1635.

THERE WAS A GREAT BATTLE IN 1625 BETWEEN THE SPANISH AND THE DUTCH AT A PLACE IN Holland called Breda. The Spanish army won the battle and here we can see the defeated Dutch general, Justin of Nassau, handing over the keys of the city of Breda to the Spanish conqueror, Spinola. The Spanish army is the one on the right of the picture, with its lances rising up to the sky like a massive steel fence. The Dutch, on the left of the painting, have no lances at all, just a few weapons called pikes. They look sad and defeated. Justin is accepting that he has lost and is behaving with dignity.

> "Please give me a loving heart that tries to understand how other people feel. Help me to be kind and sensitive and not to put myself first."

Spinola, the victor, comes to meet Justin and puts a kind hand on his shoulder. In fighting, everyone gets beaten at times and it is always painful—we are all proud and want to win. But Spinola remembers how it feels to lose and he treats Justin as he would want to be treated in defeat.

All around the two armies lies the wide world, making the battle seem a waste of time. But by treating Justin with kindness and respect, Spinola seems to be showing us how to end wars: by thinking of others before ourselves. Wars only happen when we think selfishly.

LISTENING

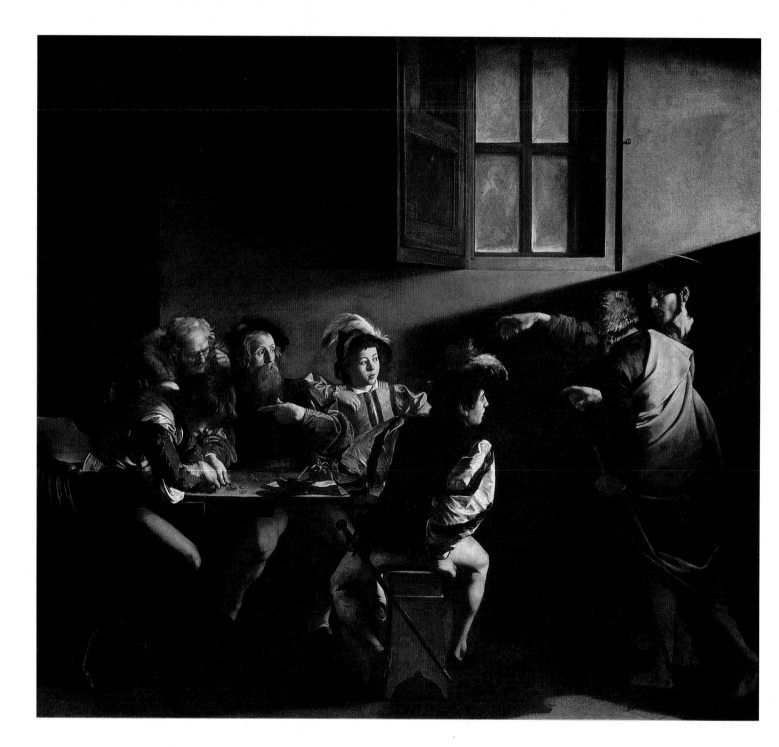

THE CALLING OF SAINT MATTHEW
Michelangelo Caravaggio
Caravaggio painted this dramatic picture
between 1599 and 1600.

HERE IS A GROUP OF MEN DOING BUSINESS IN A TAX OFFICE. THE MAN IN THE MIDDLE is Matthew, the head of the office. The door has just opened, and Jesus has appeared. He is almost hidden in shadow, but light strikes his hand as he calls to

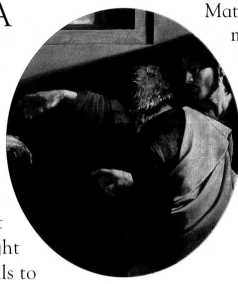

Matthew to follow him. It will mean a terrible change for Matthew. He will have to sacrifice his money and comfort and spend his life teaching people how good God is. The disciple Peter is with Jesus. His bare feet and shabby clothes show us what life as a follower of Jesus will be like.

"When I pray, I listen to you, God. Give me an ear that really hears what you are saying and help me to understand what you are asking me to do."

Jesus just points and says, "Follow me." He could be speaking to any of the other people around the table, but they do not pay attention to him. Only Matthew understands, and in the next moment, he will get up, leave everything, and become a follower of Jesus.

How tragic to miss God's call! God may have some special thing for us to do in life, but if we do not listen and look, we can miss God's call. Prayer is all about listening to God. We are all called to do something different, something that God has chosen especially for us.

PICTURE LIST

Acknowledgments

The Publisher would like to thank the following for their permission to reproduce their photographs:

l = left r = right c = center t = top b = bottom

Ashmolean Museum, Oxford 5bl (detail); 22; 23t (detail); 23b (detail); 26; 27r (detail).

Bridgeman Art Library, London: / National Gallery, London 2 (detail); 16; 17t (detail); 17b (detail); / **Prado, Madrid** 20; 21t (detail); 21b (detail); 28; 29t (detail); 29b (detail); / **Scrovegni Arena Chapel, Padua** 5tl (detail); 18; 19t (detail); 19b (detail); / **Victoria & Albert Museum, London** 7; / **Walker Art Gallery,** **Liverpool** inside cover (detail); 14; 15t (detail); 15b (detail); / **York City Art Gallery, York** 4cr; 8; 9t (detail); 9b (detail).

National Museum of Wales, Cardiff 5tr (detail); 6b (detail); 24; 25t (detail); 25b (detail).

© Photo R.M.N. / Louvre, Paris front cover / spine (detail); 10; 11t (detail); 11b (detail).

Scala / S. Luigi dei Francesi, Rome 5br (detail); 30; 31t (detail); 31b (detail).

Tate Gallery, London 1 (detail).

The Wallace Collection 3.

Woodmansterne Picture Library 12; 13t (detail); 13b (detail).